URBAN POLICY BEYOND THE NATION'S BIG METROS

Urban Policy Beyond The Nation's Big Metros
Smaller-City Case Studies from California, Washington and Michigan
Volume Nine
By Steven Greenhut, Clark S. Judge and Jeremy Lott

April 2026

ISBN: 978-1-934276-60-0

Pacific Research Institute
P.O. Box 60485
Pasadena, CA 91116

www.pacificresearch.org

URBAN POLICY BEYOND THE NATION'S BIG METROS

SMALLER-CITY CASE STUDIES FROM CALIFORNIA, WASHINGTON AND MICHIGAN

By Steven Greenhut, Clark S. Judge and Jeremy Lott

VOLUME NINE

Introduction: Urban Policy Is Not Just About Major Metros

Urban policy theorists understandably focus their attention on the major urban areas that are frequently in the news. The Free Cities Center also examines the goings-on in the nation's largest cities—with particular attention paid to Western cities—and their approach toward housing development, homelessness, transportation, crime, education and planning.

It's easy to think that urban policy is solely about big cities and their surrounding suburbs, much in the way that one would naturally believe that farm policy is solely about farm regions. A quick perusal of the statistics suggests that America is indeed an urban nation despite its vast swaths of open land and its origins as an agrarian society. The Census Bureau reports that 86% of Americans live in metropolitan areas. However, most of those metros are smaller ones.[1] A *Washington Post* analysis found that 47% of Americans live in metropolitan areas smaller than 1.5-million people. That's still a hefty percentage of the American population.[2] Around 8% of Americans live in micropolitan areas—generally small cities that serve as a hub for a rural region. There's a lot going on in those places, too.

Writing in *Strong Towns* about Staunton, Va., a 26,000-population city in the Shenandoah Valley, urbanist Addison Del Mastro, notes that this small, walkable city "is a fantastic reminder that urbanism and density do not necessarily mean big cities. The town, a form as old and hallowed as anything in America, is urban too, though it is neglected in a 'suburbs vs. cities' false dichotomy. There's no real reason why suburban population nodes—places where large highways are flanked by a couple of miles of subdivisions, hotels, strip malls, and fast food outlets—could not instead be built, at least in a denser, more walkable, and more fine-grained form."[3]

Whatever the merits of his urban-planning vision, we agree wholeheartedly with his conclusion that urbanism is not merely about big cities. Small cities, especially those that struggle more with a stagnant rather than growing population or economy, have challenges that differ from bigger cities, but innovative urban policy is important in these places, also. That idea is the genesis of this booklet. We're publishing case studies of three cities that don't spark many urban-policy headlines. It's a largely random grouping, chosen mainly because our three authors have personal knowledge of them. Their randomness actually is the point: These are nice, overlooked places of the sort where most of the American population lives. Around 85 million Americans live in the nation's 10 most-populous metropolitan areas, which leaves 255-million people living elsewhere.[4]

These three cities are Stockton, Calif., Spokane, Wash., and Hillsdale, Mich. Stockton is a useful choice for a deep dive because, with 320,000 people living there and a metro area population of 816,000, it's a rather sizable place. But it exists in the shadow of the 8-million-population San Francisco Bay Area to the west and the 2.4-million-population Sacramento area to the north. It's a blue-collar town—known for its surrounding San Joaquin Valley agricultural industry and its impressive inland port. But the city mainly makes the regional news for its crime problems. Despite these quality of life challenges, the Stockton area has been growing rapidly as Bay Area residents move there because of lower-priced real estate. Free Cities Center Director Steven Greenhut tackles this one, as he covered the city's 2012 bankruptcy and owns a house there.

Spokane is an equally illustrative case study. Like Stockton, it is fairly large. It has a population of only 230,000, but a metro area of 600,000—with a combined statistical metro population of nearly 800,000 when nearby Idaho communities such as Coeur d'Alene and Post Falls are included. Of particular interest: Spokane is fundamentally an intermountain West city that serves as the de facto capital of a vast rural and conservative region that includes northern Idaho and western Montana. Yet it is within the "blue state" of Washington, where liberal coastal cities dominate the state's politics and urban discussions. Whereas Stockton is gritty, Spokane is pastoral. Our writer, Jeremy Lott, is based in northwest Washington and has covered the state for a variety of publications.

Finally, Hillsdale is a small city—really more of a town—with a population of 8,000 and a county population of 45,000. It's in the Rust Belt and has experienced the economic disruptions that have long plagued that region as factories have moved to other regions and countries. But Hillsdale also is home to a prominent college with a nationwide reputation, which brings its own set of opportunities and challenges. Our writer, PRI chairman Clark Judge, recently moved there from Washington, D.C., so he brings a fresh perspective to small-city life after spending an impressive career in in the nation's capital as the managing director of the White House Writers Group.

This booklet's goal is to look closely at a handful of communities that are often overshadowed by the nation's most prominent cities in the hopes that they offer lessons for other cities in similar situations. We're not suggesting that there's a one-size-fits-all approach or that cities shouldn't build on their own strengths—but there are good ideas and concepts that any city could benefit from following. Whatever the solutions, we believe that those who are interested in urban ideas can glean valuable lessons from looking closely at a variety of cities of size and type.

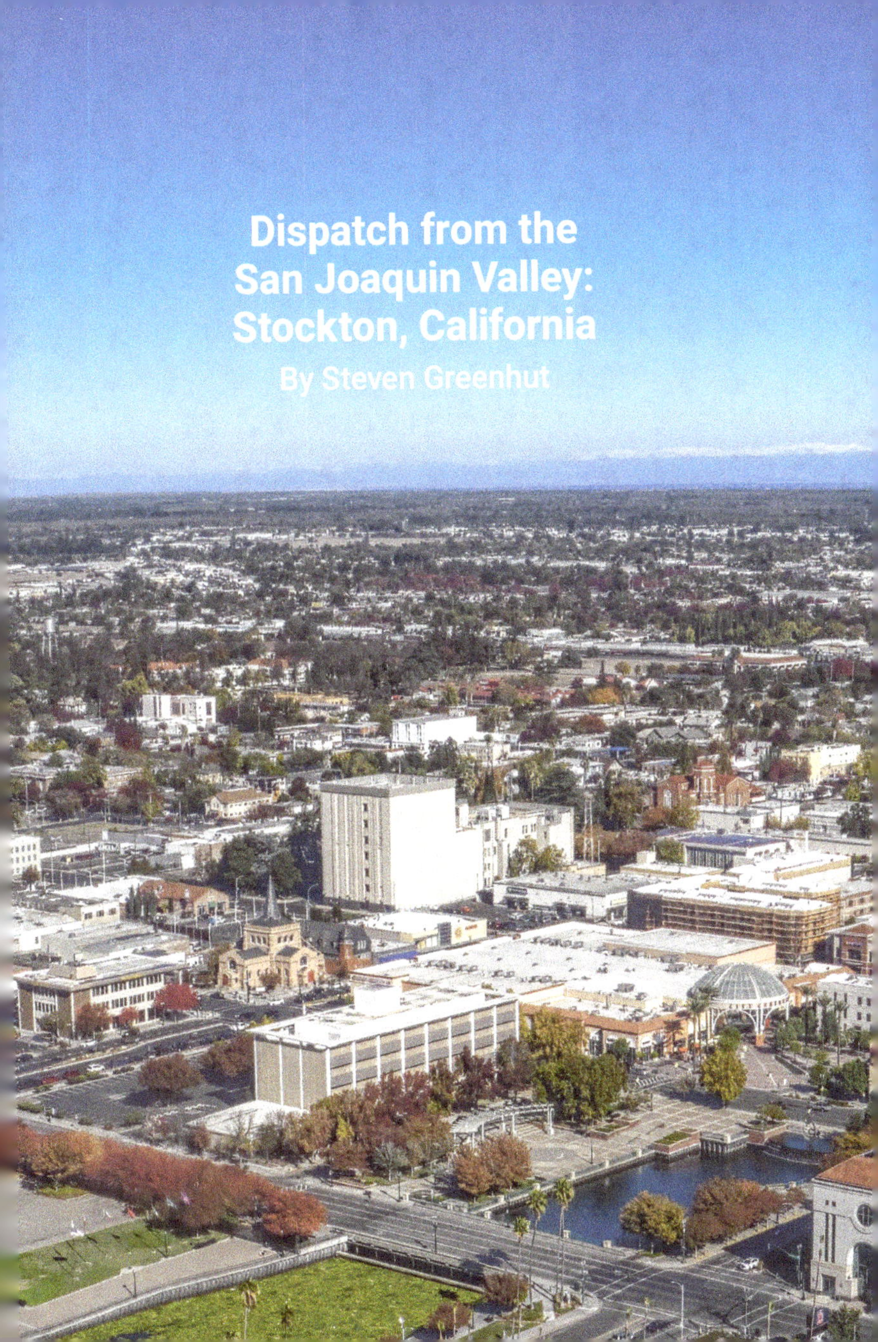

Dispatch from the
San Joaquin Valley:
Stockton, California
By Steven Greenhut

Dispatch from the San Joaquin Valley: Stockton, California

By Steven Greenhut

California's San Joaquin Valley is a vast and impressive agricultural region that spans eight counties, measuring 300 miles in length from its southern end near Bakersfield to its northern end in Lodi, just north of Stockton. It ranges in width from 40 to 60 miles, between the coastal ranges at the west to the Sierra Nevada foothills to the east. The valley floor—home to the nation's most-productive and varied agriculture—is larger than the state of Maryland. It's not the California that most out-of-staters think about, with its flat landscapes and big, open sky. It has a hefty population of 4.5-million people, but most Californians who live in the state's Southern California and Bay Area megalopolises think of the valley mostly as the boring stretch one drives through from Los Angeles to San Francisco.

The land along Interstate 5 is mostly empty, but more adventurous travelers will travel via the 99 freeway, which bisects most valley cities from Bakersfield to Tulare to Fresno to Merced to Modesto. Those who take that trek veer west to the Bay Area by taking 120 in Manteca, just south of the city of Stockton. There's no understanding Stockton without understanding this big, beautiful valley.[5]

The San Joaquin Valley is defined by its agriculture, of course. I still enjoy reading its depiction by a *New York Times* journalist who helicoptered in 14 years ago:

> There is a gritty majesty to San Joaquin, the southern half of California's Central Valley. Route 99, the freeway that bisects it, thunders with the traffic of tractor-trailers that haul equipment in and agricultural products out 24/7. The geography beside the highway is marked by grain elevators and storage silos that soar like medieval turrets. Enormous piles of almond hulls (sold as cattle feed) rise in conical mounds as tall as five-story buildings. I passed warehouse after warehouse, each big enough to be an airplane hangar. Farm equipment dealerships broke up monotonous gray and whites with the yellow, green, orange, and scarlet hues of tractors, plows, combines, dump trucks, bulldozers and Rube Goldberg contraptions whose purpose I could only guess, all seemingly designed to be operated by a race of giants.[6]

The valley is Ground Zero for the state's water wars given that California's agriculture industry uses 40% of the state's water and often has to fight big cities for more of it. It's still home to a bustling oil-and-gas industry, especially in the lower reaches of Kern County. It's also a place where many residents still don't have access to potable water.

"The eight-county San Joaquin Valley, part of California's Central Valley, is home to five of the 10 most agriculturally productive counties in the United States," per a 2005 Congressional Research Service report," and it "is also one of the most economically depressed regions of the United States." CRS even compares it to impoverished Appalachia.[7]

It's against that backdrop that one needs to understand the city of Stockton, which is the third largest city in the San Joaquin Valley (and the fourth largest in the Central Valley). It is fundamentally a valley city even though the Census Bureau now considers it part of the San Jose-San Francisco-Oakland Combined Statistical Area given that so many people commute from the Stockton area into the eastern portions of the Bay Area. If you drive around Stockton, it looks like an old industrial city, with a neglected historic downtown, grain silos and all the industrial accoutrements of its giant port. It's not a long drive over the Altamont Pass into the affluent suburbs that ring San Francisco, but outside of a few neighborhoods and shopping centers, the city lacks that area's affluent and modern vibe.

Stockton's Strange Politics

The city also has a rough-and-tumble way about it, with its politics far removed from the progressive hothouses 85 miles to the west or at the Capitol 40 miles north. A May 2013 CBS News report captured one particularly odd phase in the city's political turmoil, as then-Mayor Anthony Silva gave his State of the City address: "'Who's willing? If you are willing, stand up and show me you are willing to fight for the city,' said Silva. After his almost hour-long speech, Silva pulled out armor with a helmet and mace while asking the crowd to go to war for the broke and crime-ridden city."[8] Silva focused his attention on hiring more police and on a variety of law-and-order themes as it struggled with a crime wave and its recent financial insolvency.

Silva lost re-election in 2016 by a 70% to 30% vote after a series of bizarre scandals,[9] but the incoming mayor was odd in a different way. The new mayor, Michael Tubbs, who was at the time a young Democratic activist who made headlines for his attention-grabbing progressive approach to governance—something rather alien to the relatively conservative city's history. Consider this 2017 NBC News headline: "Stockton Mayor Considers Adopting Program That Pays Criminals Not To Shoot People."[10] Tubbs was savaged for his "cash for criminals" program. His other controversial idea, which received nationwide praise and derision, was to create a privately funded Universal Basic Income program that paid 125 Stockton residents $500 a month to use any way they saw fit.[11]

Despite Tubbs' heavy salesmanship promoting the program, there's no evidence that it worked. As PRI's analysis found, "40 percent of the money on the prepaid debit cards (offered to participants) were transferred to bank accounts or withdrawn as cash," which PRI economist Dr. Wayne Winegarden argued makes "any conclusions about the efficacy (or inefficacy) of a UBI impossible to draw."[12]

As former pro football player turned entrepreneur and think tank scholar Damon Dunn wrote in his PRI book *Punting Poverty*, basic income programs like Tubbs' initiative are "fool's gold that do not even attempt to offer economic empowerment."[13]

At age 29 and with few tangible policy successes, Tubbs was nevertheless featured in an 89-minute HBO documentary about his efforts to turn around the city. He spent time on the speaker circuit. Oprah Winfrey donated to his campaign.[14] "For young Democrats, Tubbs had served as a model of how quickly an ambitious and charismatic candidate, even with little political experience, could gain power in a major American city, and use that seat to advance progressive causes across the country," *Politico* reported[15] in 2020, after Tubbs lost his re-election bid 56% to 44% to Marine veteran Kevin Lincoln, a Republican. Lincoln, who is now running for Congress, focused on traditional urban issues of crime and homelessness, with some degree of success. Tubbs is now running for lieutenant governor.

Here is *Politico* quoting Bob Benedetti, a retired professor from the nearby University of the Pacific: "Tubbs had an external network—these people who thought he was an up-and-comer, but he had no internal network, and he never created one. He didn't put together a team of local clubs or local organizations who would trumpet his success."[16] He's certainly not the first politician who forgot former House Speaker Tip O'Neill's quip that all politics is local by spending more time enjoying the national spotlight than overseeing departments that fixed potholes and enforced local codes.

San Joaquin County is solidly Democratic and Democrats hold a more than two-to-one voter registration advantage in Stockton,[17] but this is a blue-collar valley city where traditional law-enforcement and economic-development themes are far more popular than progressive pipedreams. Its politics also reveal a refreshing lack of partisanship. Voters are willing to vote for candidates from either party. I've chatted with Jesus Andrade, a pragmatic Republican who once represented the city's poorest council district. The current mayor, Christina Fugazi, is a Democrat who embraces mainstream policies. She says that she "played a key role in guiding Stockton out of bankruptcy, restoring police staffing and securing funding to combat urban blight, including a 'broken windows' grant for commercial restoration."[18]

But even with a more reasonable political turn, Stockton faces some intractable problems that are tied to its industrial economic base, the poverty endemic in the region, poor choices made by previous political leadership and its location not far from the edge of a sprawling and entirely different type of metropolitan region, where issues center more on AI development than shipping. And there's no escaping Stockton's struggles to overcome the city's failed past decision making. Bad leadership has consequences and Stockton is a case study in that realm.

Stockton Goes Bankrupt

In 2012, Stockton became the largest city in the United States to file for Chapter 9 bankruptcy protection, although much-larger Detroit followed in 2013. City officials blamed the fallout from the 2008 subprime mortgage crisis, as the real-estate housing bubble burst. They weren't entirely wrong in their explanation, as Stockton was particularly hard hit by the crisis. Because of soaring home prices in the San Francisco Bay Area, Stockton's housing prices increased rapidly as long-distance commuters flocked to the area. As we saw during that time, prices tumbled the most in communities that were farthest from the main jobs centers given that they lacked the economic fundamentals to sustain the higher prices. Prices fell, for instance, by 16% in San Francisco but by far more in Stockton.[19] Here's a 2012 summary from the Reason Foundation:

The housing bust decimated Stockton's housing prices, and so went the city's property tax (and related) revenues. Housing prices plunged from nearly $400,000 in median home prices in 2006, down to $110,000 in 2009 (where median prices were in 2000 before the bubble.) Meanwhile the city has the second highest rate of foreclosures in the country. Revenues from related areas, such as sales taxes, utility user's taxes and housing permit fees, also plunged.[20]

I recall those times personally. I purchased a 1930s bungalow near Stockton's main city park, Victory Park, for $78,000—at 23 cents on the dollar from the property's sale price at the height of price escalation. Every street was filled with for sale signs, mostly foreclosures. The banks could barely give away those properties at the time. These were depressing times. The online foreclosure listings were enormous—and not just in Stockton but in inland areas throughout the Central Valley as well as Southern California's Inland Empire and High Desert communities. I remember one news story from Mountain House, a new subdivision just east of the coastal ranges near Tracy, about a builder who slashed prices $100,000 on existing inventory. These price drops stressed even the best-run cities.

But, alas, Stockton was not a best-run city. *Reuters* produced some of the best reporting on the bankruptcy during the time in its piece about Stockton's "15-year spending binge." Per the article: "As the 2000s advanced, Stockton continued to spend freely with the support of voters, politicians from both parties, employees and bondholders. Rating agencies were quiet about any risks and only started to downgrade the city's creditworthiness (in 2010)."[21] It quoted former city manager Bob Deis, who pointed specifically to the city's decision to give firefighters full healthcare benefits in retirement. Then other unions demanded and received the same benefit in the usual one-way ratchet.

I attended some of Stockton's bankruptcy proceedings at the federal courthouse in Sacramento, where one city official described that health plan as a "Lamborghini-style"[22] benefit whereby employees and their family members could receive lifetime healthcare after working for the city for a few months. And then the city went all in on the lavish "3% at 50" pension plan for public-safety workers that guaranteed them and their spouses 90% or more of their highest salary for the rest of their lives. City pay packages were at 125% of statewide averages[23] even though Stockton was a relatively low-cost place. The city, which is older than San Francisco and has a treasure trove of historic buildings and parks, saw its infrastructure decline as the city squandered its funds on pay packages.

Then-Councilwoman Kathy Miller explained the predicament in a video she produced for local residents: "Stockton went even further than most other cities and granted things like unlimited vacation and sick time that could be cashed out when an employee retired, and added pay categories for almost everything imaginable. … Our public safety employees were costing us on average more than $150,000 a year each. That's three times more than most of us in Stockton make in a year."[24]

The city began slashing its spending before heading to bankruptcy court, but it was too little, too late. At the time, the core argument in court was whether the city could abrogate its pension promises in the face of a bankruptcy. Essentially, Stockton chose to stiff its creditors rather than fix its fundamental spending problems. In approving the bankruptcy, Judge Christopher

Klein nevertheless offered some good news for pension reformers: He declared that the city could reduce its pension promises during bankruptcy, even though California law protected public employees' full pensions. Despite the latitude the court offered, the city decline to shave these pensions, although it did cut some non-vested benefits such as healthcare.

In the ensuing years, Stockton raised taxes three times, thus making the city less competitive economically with neighboring communities. In 2018, the watchdog group Truth In Accounting placed Stockton on a national list of financially healthy cities, joining the upscale Orange County city of Irvine as the only two California mid-sized cities to receive the honor.[25] That was encouraging news on the surface, but largely just a function of Stockton's tax profligacy as the group mainly looks at debt issues. But while higher taxes can plug budget holes, they also discourage business growth and inequitably burden taxpayers. Even by that metric, by 2023, Truth in Accounting gave Stockton a "C" grade for its financial health and it's remained in a similar position since.[26] The city is in stable shape, a far cry from its 2012 disaster. But it's hard not to speculate about how much better its infrastructure could be had the city taken a more prudent fiscal path.

As former Stockton Assembly member Dean Andal, a Republican, told me at the time: "We have much higher taxes and much lower service levels than before the bankruptcy. We get to pay more for less and the tax revenue goes to pensions."[27] There's got to be a better way to move forward, especially for a city with a backlog of infrastructure needs.

Stockton's Redevelopment Boondoggles

One of the infrequently discussed aspects of Stockton's past fiscal crisis was a policy that ties directly to its urban-uplift visions. Like many second-tier cities, Stockton repeatedly sought to make itself a destination by employing various economic-development techniques that subsidized sports teams and other downtown projects. I've covered these types of projects throughout my career, in upscale communities and downtrodden ones. Occasionally, the projects pan out—such as in San Diego's Gaslamp Quarter or in Old Town Pasadena. But redevelopment projects often result in vacant lots, dashed promises, underutilized facilities and debt—lots of it. The latter is most common in cities that have few natural attractions and struggling economies.[28]

Shortly after the city declared bankruptcy, former Stockton resident Jim Conn, writing in *Capital & Main*, touched on that part of the city's failings as he decried the city's "urban redevelopment by bulldozer, tax rebates for businesses that didn't need them, city planning run by developers, (and) municipal bonds for projects that promised a future built on illusions."[29] Stockton wasn't the only city to use the state's now-shuttered redevelopment agencies in such a way. California's 1940s-era urban-renewal program allowed localities to create these agencies. City officials targeted areas for redevelopment, floated debt, subsidized developers and then grabbed the tax increment—the increase in property taxes after the project was complete—to pay off the debt. They sought to enliven decrepit areas and to collect sales taxes from the completed projects.

The system rarely worked as planned and the state mercifully disbanded redevelopment agencies in 2013, given that the property tax diversions came at the expense of traditional public services and the state budget. Stockton's downtown redevelopment projects—a minor-league baseball park, hockey arena, marina and downtown hotel and entertainment area—contributed mightily to the city's debt. Those projects never created the predicted downtown revival even if they bring some downtown energy on game day. As *Reuters* reported, city officials at the time pitched the downtown projects as a way to lure more people from the Bay Area. Some of those projects have remained in litigation between the city and developers for decades. The city often did more bulldozing than building, thus decimating its historic building stock. It's a common story when city officials are given the power to make development decisions.

Those public investments were driven by some of the same types of economic disruptions common in the Rust Belt. In Stockton's case, the federal government closed a naval base. Its manufacturing economy had long been declining. "Like Baltimore, San Diego and numerous post-industrial waterfront cities before it, Stockton got itself a family-friendly downtown, including a heavily subsidized waterfront development and hotel, new sports stadiums and a suburban-style megaplex with an IMAX theater and shops," explained *Next City*.[30] This is from a 2012 article in *Bloomberg*:

> In 2005, Stockton, Calif., unveiled a gleaming sports arena on its waterfront, part of a $145 million plan to draw people downtown. The 10,000-seat facility, a glass-walled symbol of the city's battle against downtown blight, was part of a redevelopment boom that also saw the addition of a 5,000-seat minor league ballpark, a 650-space parking garage, a 66-

slip marina, and the purchase of an eight-story City Hall. 'This is the project that's going to bring folks home, and it's going to bring people from around the region to Stockton,' then-council member Leslie Martin said in 2004 when the waterfront revival was approved. The building boom was financed with a series of bond issues starting in 2003 that helped boost Stockton's debt load to $977 million.[31]

It didn't turn out as planned. The city only recently started vacating its decrepit but beautiful historic City Hall, with the cost of its new City Hall project having tripled.[32] The hotel project was also a bust as there was little demand for overnight stays downtown. The owners turned many of its rooms into dormitories for the University of the Pacific, a short drive north of downtown.[33] The city allowed historic buildings to fall into disrepair and they become magnets for homeless encampments. The downtown remains decrepit and largely vacant, although the echoes remain of what once existed in the city's heyday. One can squint and still envision what could still be a vibrant place.

Perennial Struggles with Crime

At the time of the bankruptcy, Stockton was facing a crime surge that only enhanced the sense of a dying city. Here in the Sacramento area, people often view it as a dangerous place to be avoided at all costs. The situation isn't as bad as the perception, at least it doesn't feel that way unless you're in one of the blighted neighborhoods south of the 4 freeway. The region's TV stations are based in the capital city, so the main stories we learn about Stockton involve the latest horrendous crime that took place. I spend time in the city and despite its reputation, it has many beautiful historic neighborhoods with local bars and restaurants. But the crime statistics don't lie. When the city was trying to get its spending under control in 2010, the city's police union bought billboards across town depicting blood splatter and stating: "Welcome to the 2nd most dangerous city in California—Stop laying off cops."[34] The council's dispute with the union certainly didn't help the city's reputation.

After a mass shooting at a Stockton birthday party in December 2025 that left four people dead including three children,[35] local and state officials once again have tried to step up their efforts to handle the city's seemingly intractable violent-crime problem. Not much has changed in overall rankings since 2010 even as the city's finances have improved, with Stockton routinely near the top of the state's list of crime centers—only Oakland (currently at risk of bankruptcy), Vallejo (which went bankrupt in 2008) and San Bernardino (which went bankrupt in 2012) give it a run for the money. Stockton's homicide rate did drop significantly in 2025 from the previous year, which has offered some encouragement—but theft rates remained stubbornly high. In December, Gov. Gavin Newsom announced a state program[36] designed specifically to battle gang-related crime in the city, so we'll see if the renewed attention will yield measurable results.

Meanwhile, the city's housing market has rebounded to the point where high home prices are again a mounting concern. The median home price is $420,000—roughly double median prices in 2012, and still a pittance of prices in the Bay Area. By contrast, Sacramento's median home price is $475,000, Oakland's is $684,000 and San Jose is $1.4 million.[37] There's still plenty of financial incentive for people to move to Stockton, even if it still can't get the governing fundamentals right.

Why Would Anyone Move There?

Forgive me for providing such a bleak review of the city, but civic improvement must spring from an honest appraisal of the situation. To answer the above question: My wife and I actuallyly considered moving there and looked at and put in offers on a handful of properties. We ultimately decided to buy a house in an older suburb of Sacramento, but the reasons were mostly unrelated to the current problems facing the city. They factored in, of course. My wife was somewhat uncomfortable with the shabby condition of many Stockton parks—and I've repeatedly been frustrated with the lack of responsiveness from city officials on issues involving my rental property's neighborhood. But we like the city and I know many Stockton residents who remain committed to it.

Stockton has its charms. It has many lovely, leafy neighborhoods, access to parks and waterways, a fine private university with a campus that looks straight out of New England, and a dogged sense of community pride. It feels like a real place. As someone who grew up on the East Coast, I appreciate the strange beauty of a city where tanker ships, derricks, grain silos and impressive buildings dominate the landscape. And despite the hike in home prices, one can still buy a fabulous old home for a fraction of what it would cost elsewhere in Northern California. Despite ugly sprawl to the north and south, the city quickly turns into the Delta estuary to the west and the foothills of the Sierra Nevada Mountains to the east. Throw in its mild climate and there's no reason Stockton shouldn't be thriving.

What Can City Officials Do?

California, for all its merits, often serves as a case study for what other states ought not to do. Likewise, Stockton—and especially the pre-bankruptcy Stockton—is often a case study in what policies to avoid. But Stockton and other cities need to focus on three fundamentals.

First, cities need to build sustainable budgets. That's tough when public-sector unions have so much power to make demands and elect council members who give in to them. Council members must be willing to say no, even if unions pepper the city with repulsive billboards. There's no easy button solution to this endless democratic problem. It's the same conundrum faced by cities everywhere, including highly sophisticated and affluent cities in the Los Angeles basin and the Bay Area. But poorer and financially strapped ones don't have the breathing room to get it wrong. There's no getting around reality, however. Reviving older, hard-scrabble cities starts with the basics: keep the budget under control so that the tax rates don't chase away businesses and existing tax revenues can improve infrastructure.

Second, cities need to provide excellent public services. In the well-run suburban city where I live, my neighbor called the police department because of a speeding problem on our street and the next day a motorcycle officer showed up with a radar gun. That inspires confidence. When I write to my city officials here, I get a response. When I repeatedly contacted Stockton officials about a tree issue, I didn't even get a pro forma response. When my tenant called the Stockton police department about a possible break in next door, the police said they wouldn't even respond. Even cities with pressing crime problems—and perhaps especially in those cities—need to develop a responsive system that inspires confidence in its residents. Residents remain a core tool in crime fighting, after all. Stockton has spent tens of millions of dollars on those previously mentioned redevelopment projects, yet many city owned buildings are in disrepair. This is not a financial issue so much as a municipal priority and competence issue.

Third, instead of focusing on high-cost economic-development projects that require bonds and massive subsidies, cities need to encourage private-sector investments and ground-up development projects driven by residents and investors rather than City Hall bureaucrats and rent-seeking developers. Even with the demise of redevelopment agencies, cities still can misuse subsidies and eminent domain to benefit private developers. It's not as easy as without them, but California lawmakers never seriously reformed their economic-development laws following the Supreme Court's 2005 *Kelo* decision allowing eminent domain for public-benefit projects.

Successful cities can use market-oriented tools to accomplish the same goals without giving a heavy hand to planners who pick economic winners and losers. For a short time, the city of Anaheim in 2006 embraced a "freedom friendly Anaheim" approach that upzoned properties and essentially reduced zoning requirements, thus allowing private developers to build major projects on previously restricted sites.[38] The city also streamlined its permitting process. While Stockton's downtown remains in shambles, it has many lovely neighborhood businesses and shopping centers. Instead of thinking big, city officials ought to start small. What makes those restaurants and pubs so successful? This reinforces my point about getting the fundamentals right: If the city could get control of its crime problem, more people will move and invest there. It will improve the quality of life for everyone. Ditto if the school district improved its educational performance.

As part of its Free Cities Center booklet series on urban issues and other Pacific Research Institute studies and books, we've found that some of these concepts help bolster the fundamentals:

- Regarding crime, cities need to create responsive, community-oriented police departments that engage the public in this difficult task. They need to reform their pension and compensation systems so they can afford to hire the necessary number of officers.

- Regarding homelessness, cities need to embrace the latitude that the U.S. Supreme Court provided in its 2024 *Grants Pass* decision and clear away homeless encampments from public parks and property. Some cities have succeeded by eschewing "Housing First" policies and instead building homeless facilities that offer wraparound services.

- Regarding housing, cities need to permit more housing developments, upzone properties and focus on untying the hands of market-rate developers rather than subsidizing affordable housing or imposing counterproductive rent controls.

- Regarding transportation, cities need to put customers first, by creating efficiently run transit systems that cater to commuters rather than hectoring drivers to abandon their cars.

- Regarding education, urban school districts need to emphasize charter schools and other forms of educational choice.

The answers always involve creativity, partnerships, private-sector involvement and competition. They sometimes require the city and its bureaucracies to get out of the way or reform the way they operate. It all starts with a municipality that understands that a thriving city economically is rooted in the people who live there. It requires an understanding that city governments are there to primarily serve their residents rather than the people who work for the city. Leadership must recognize the challenge—and be willing to innovate and bring its own fiscal and bureaucratic structures up to snuff. That's not a challenge unique to Stockton, but it would be so exciting if such a beautiful and interesting place rose to the occasion.

Dispatch from the Intermountain West: Spokane, Washington
By Jeremy Lott
WASHINGTON

Dispatch from the Intermountain West: Spokane, Washington

By Jeremy Lott

Spokane is Washington state's second city behind Seattle, by population and especially influence. Tacoma is close in numbers, with just over 228,000 residents[39] to Spokane's over 230,000,[40] according to the World Population Review. Even if Tacoma were to shoot past Spokane numerically, it is part of Seattle's metro area, with no real way to escape the Emerald City's shadow.

Spokane has some distance and even occasionally some swagger. Its prominence was on glorious display in late June 2025, during a visit there to attend a funeral and memorial service. The same weekend that I flew in to remember my late godmother, a longtime Spokane resident, the city hosted Hoopfest, an annual event that boasts of being the "largest 3on3 basketball tournament on Earth." Its closest competition is probably the Nike Basketball 3on3 tournament in Los Angeles.[41]

The typical team of the 6,000 or so teams that participate puts up $120 to $220 in entry fees, depending on age and other factors. That money goes to finance the tournament and the other work of the Hoopfest Association, as players aren't competing for a pot. They win bragging rights along with free t-shirts to reinforce that bragging.

There were plenty of other things than Hoopfest that we saw that weekend. In our free time, we visited the Northwest Museum of Arts and Culture, aka the MAC, got lost driving around in neighborhoods that seemed to be a wildflower mix of Victorian homes and more modern styles of housing, and tried several different local coffee shops, restaurants and local reading material. Spokane has a great daily newspaper in the *Spokesman-Review* and one of the few still-standing alt-weeklies in *The Inlander*.

The *Spokesman-Review* covers stories from angles that many other papers might overlook. For instance, it is not intuitive that 800-plus injuries in a weekend would be cause for celebration, but reporter Corbin Vanderby pointed out that it's actually well below the tournament's average casualty rate.

"Hoopfest nets over 800 injuries, down from previous years," the headline read.[42]

Here are some other things Spokane is known for:

- Its massive Riverfront Park that includes Spokane Falls, an ice skating rink, a cable car ride, evening light shows, sculptures, a carousel and a 12-foot high Radio Flyer Wagon;[43]
- The Bing Crosby Theater, a grand refurbished stage for the performing arts that celebrates a local boy made good;
- A huge number of beautiful historic buildings and quirky landmarks, including the magnificent and renovated Historic Davenport Hotel, the Glover Mansion, St. John's Cathedral and the Benewah Milk Bottle Building;

- Enough breweries and brewpubs to attract serious beer tourists;
- The Lilac Bloomsday Run each May;
- The Gonzaga Bulldogs, highly competitive in the world of college basketball;
- And believe it or not, Father's Day.

That celebration was created by the late Sonora Smart Dodd. The story goes, she listened to a Mother's Day sermon and decided that her own widower father, who raised six children, deserved a day as well. She managed to convince the Spokane and Washington state governments to declare the holiday, and it caught on nationally.[44]

Any time you move one inch away from politics, you can see that Spokane is a city with a storied past and a lot going for it in the present. This is what locals refer to as "the better Spokane." But there's a worse Spokane, too.

Homeless Encampment Echoes *Lord of the Flies*

Lord of the Flies is a gripping novel. A plane crash strands a group of English schoolboys alone on a deserted island during wartime. The pilot dies in the crash.

The accident leaves the boys to fend for themselves. They do their best to recreate the rule-based order of their parents while that order battles an existential threat. However, they do not meet the challenge. Things break down, and they break badly. The boys revert to savagery and even murder, with a lingering shame that will overshadow the survivors' lives.

Still widely assigned in American schools today, *SparkNotes* calls *Lord of the Flies* "a powerful exploration of the inherent capacity for savagery within human beings when societal structures are removed."

Astonishingly, it can also apply to city services. Consider a huge, multiyear homeless encampment in East Central Spokane that was only cleared after an extended struggle by politicians, lawyers and law enforcement.

When asked about the situation, Jeffry Finer, at the time a lawyer for Jewels Helping Hands, a local charity contracted by the state to work in that encampment of several hundred homeless, said, "If [the encampment] turned into *Lord of the Flies*, it was pushed that way." [45] [46]

Jewels assisted many homeless who had illegally camped out on highway access land owned by the Washington State Department of Transportation. It was one of several parties that litigated on their behalf.[47]

Finer argues that an alleged lack of resources from law enforcement and the wider community had made conditions in the camp worse for those who squatted there.

The comparison between camp conditions is not out of line. Between December 2021 to June 2023, conditions at the camp included drug activity, property crime, reckless burning, auto theft, rape, harassment, burglary and threats to public health, as reported by the local TV station KREM2.[48] One man was allegedly branded with the equivalent of a hot poker— in this case, a heated piece of metal rebar—over a drug deal gone south.[49]

The situation only ended after police and firefighters were called to the scene because of a loud explosion and fire in the early morning of March 17, 2023. Two homeless people were rushed to the hospital with extensive burns.

Investigators determined that those two campers "were trans-filling propane tanks in the tent where a propane heater was already operating," according to the *Spokesman-Review*. "Propane leaked out while transferring the gas, filling the tent with it and causing the explosion and fire."[50]

That was enough for a federal judge to finally end the encampment, whose name I have obscured until this point because it cuts so sharply against the actual reported experience there. One week after the explosion, the mayor's office of Spokane announced that a judge had finally declared Camp Hope to be "a public health and safety hazard [and] a nuisance, and ordered the state to work with the City on a plan to clear it."[51]

Housing First or Housing Worst?

The Camp Hope experience is representative of many problems the de facto capital of eastern Washington faces. As we will see, the city's experience with homelessness also has broader relevance for the recent difficulties many American cities have been having in navigating the issue as well.

Homelessness in Spokane had not been a significant problem because of the city's geography. It has some elevation, with an average height approaching 2,000 feet above sea level, as well as nearby mountains. Compared to coastal western Washington, Spokane has summers that are often very hot and winters that can be brutally, punishingly cold. Most people use shelter and its related features, including air conditioning and indoor heating, to moderate those conditions.

Spokane's homeless have a much harder go of it than they would if they lived on the other side of the state, with its more temperate climate. Thus the local remedies had typically been more geared towards getting those few people without shelter treatment for the things that tend to cause or exacerbate homelessness, principally drug addiction and serious mental illness.

In Spokane and elsewhere, the U.S. federal government came to disapprove of this approach. "In 2013, the federal government adopted a 'Housing First' policy that prohibits participation requirements in programs receiving federal funding," wrote Robert G. Marbut Jr., former executive director of the U.S. Interagency Council on Homelessness, in a June 2025 report for the Spokane Business Association.[52]

The idea behind Housing First is to get homeless people housing and worry about the underlying reasons for their homelessness, such as drug addiction, alcoholism, mental-health issues or criminal behavior, later. But this involves tradeoffs and cities almost never have the funds or the capability to quickly build housing. As a result, any housing tends to happen very slowly. In the meantime, the causes of homelessness go untreated or under-treated.

The federal shift in turn routed funding "away from wraparound services such as substance use treatment or job training programs" and thus "created serious gaps in care for individuals with substance use disorder and mental illness," Marbut wrote. He granted that "stability and recovery are more achievable when a person is housed," yet insisted that the "dogmatic application of Housing First has too often come at the expense of treatment and supportive services that make enduring recovery possible."

Further, a majority of the current homeless in Spokane have little or no historical connection to the city. This means that they typically have no private support networks to help out in a pinch. This lack of connection only prolongs the time folks spend unsheltered, and increases their agony.

Marbut conducted a survey which found that "63.2% of the [homeless] population reported never having family ties to Spokane, 73.5% did not attend high school in Spokane and 80.7% were born outside of Spokane." In fact, just over half of the measured homeless population, or 50.2%, "first began experiencing homelessness outside of Spokane, then moved to Spokane."

And they can expect to stay homeless for a lot longer there. Marbut found that the locals surveyed, "have been experiencing homelessness for an average of 8.7 years." And yes this length of time on the streets is "extremely high" and in fact much worse than what we see in Seattle, which has an average of only 4.2 years per person.

There was a recent slight drop in the homeless population according to the 2025 point-in-time count,[53] but it is distressingly possible that has less to do with housing and more to do with the uptick of drug- and specifically fentanyl-related deaths. The report warned that if "nothing dramatically changes, Spokane's unsheltered population will likely continue to grow rapidly in the coming years," which would be bad for public safety, public finances and especially bad for the homeless themselves.

The Problem of Polarization

The cause underlying many of Spokane's problems including the homelessness struggle is what social scientists call polarization. Polarization can go beyond simple and understandable partisan divides on some issues. Party, ideology and allegiance to a larger movement become all-consuming—so much so that these often override local needs and local knowledge.

Spokane elects non-partisan officeholders, not Republicans or Democrats, to city government. Nevertheless, we have seen the ill effects of polarization on many issues in Spokane over the last several years. For instance, the City Council pushed the Spokane Police Department toward a fleet with more electric vehicles, notwithstanding the facts that EVs perform poorly in cold weather and that Teslas and other EVs are not optimized for police usage.[54]

Another example: The Spokane City Council nonpartisan progressive majority became so obsessed with the state government's extensive masking policies that they voted to censure one city councilor who unmasked in certain instances and asked the mayor to expel him from City Hall.[55]

On spending, the Spokane City Council's nonpartisan progressive majority pushed its own priorities at the expense of the city's long-term fiscal health. This helped worsen a funding shortage this year of about $13 million, and led to the following suboptimal employment scenario, described by the progressive news outlet *RANGE Media*:[56]

"If your boss was holding a public meeting about whether you should be laid off, would you want to know? On Veteran's Day [2025], Spokane City Council staffers weren't given the option after they were kicked out of just such a meeting—an open, public one — by council members who preferred to discuss firing them behind their backs."

For a long time, those standing in the way of that polarized vision on homelessness, such as former nonpartisan Spokane Major Nadine Woodward and nonpartisan former Spokane city and county police chiefs Craig Meidl and Ozzie Knezovich, were pushed or eased out of office.

In the face of this, Spokane voters showed some spine. They overwhelmingly passed Proposition 1 to ban urban camping near parks and schools in November 2023. Jewels, of *Lord of the Flies* fame, challenged it in court and the Washington State Supreme Court eventually threw the law out a few years later. The U.S. Supreme Court's *Grants Pass* decision had made it easier for municipalities to enact such laws, but the Washington State Supreme Court was undeterred, declaring that the measure "exceeds the proper scope of the local initiative power."[57]

After Polarization: Yes We Spokane!

There are also some happy signs that polarization may be slowly breaking down. One thing Spokane has going for it is property values that have not risen high enough to price many younger buyers out of the market, as has happened in much of western Washington.

The median sale price for a home in the state in November 2025 was $626,300[58], but only $380,000[59] in Spokane, according to figures from Redfin. Moreover, the Spokane government is doing things to encourage the building of more housing and more types of housing to ensure affordability. Some of the building code changes[60] that went into effect at the beginning of 2024 include:

- Design standards for single-unit detached homes and Middle Housing developments;
- No parking required for residential uses within half a mile of a transit stop;

- No lot density maximums for lots less than two acres in size;
- Reduced lot size minimums;
- Expanded Unit Lot Subdivision process to allow for greater site flexibility; and
- Increased building height and reduced front and rear setbacks for some zones.

This all adds up to more flexibility for builders to build more types of buildings and more densely than historic single-family zoning had allowed. It also vastly scales back parking requirements that cost a great deal of money in many cities.

Economic development professional Anthony Gill praised the new parking flexibility. He showed how it might appeal to some progressives and then made the case in *The Urbanist* for why the "libertarian-minded" should like it as well:

> [O]ptional parking gives property owners a choice. If off-street parking would be necessary to rent or sell a unit, then the market will respond and that off-street parking will still be provided. But say, for example, an individual property owner wants to build a new home but doesn't own a car or want to own one. Previously they would have been required by the city to construct a parking stall even if they didn't even own a car. Even worse, it is illegal for landlords to charge renters less if they don't have a car. This optional parking ordinance remedies that injustice.[61]

Also, chalk this one up to a change of heart or the political expediency of not wanting to defy a 75% majority, but the Spokane City Council finally moved on the homeless issue. It passed the "Safe and Accessible Spaces" ordinance at the end of October 2025 unanimously.[62]

The bill gives Spokane PD a series of carrots, sticks and carroty sticks. It authorizes officers "to offer assistance to willing individuals, issue citations to rule-breakers, or do both," as the existing law on that subject was "viewed as unclear."

According to the city, the new ordinance widens the scope of what counts as illegal obstruction to include "any portion of public property" and specifically calls out bridges, stairways, medians, plazas and transit facilities. No longer will those cited for unlawful public burning, a potential lethal hazard, automatically be "cited and released" by law. It also adds harsher penalties for repeat offenders and seeks to give police broad powers to discourage camping and obstruction on all public spaces, "including rights-of-way and entry points to private properties."

The unanimity of support for this legislation was so rare that the city noted it in a news release, calling this, "the first time in recent memory that all seven City Council members have formally sponsored an ordinance." Council President Betsy Wilkerson declared that the bill's "historic bipartisan support demonstrates that we can transcend differences and prioritize the needs of our entire community."

Where Spokane Goes From Here

There is general agreement that putting more police on the streets of Spokane could help, at the margin, to lower crime. There is also consternation that the city doesn't have the money for it. Enter the U.S. Department of Justice with its Community Oriented Policing Services (COPS) program.

Through the COPS program, the federal government agreed to cough up $1 million over five years to help hire eight new officers.[63] It may or may not have been a deal worth making, because the grant didn't fully fund those officers. But the Spokane City Council's hand-wringing over it, because it could require some minimal cooperation with the federal government on the issue of illegal immigration, was 1) not helpful, and 2) a very Seattle reaction.

The Spokane city government is making some great moves on housing that should help with affordability. These actions are in concert with a statewide push for more urban density, to a degree. Yet local elected officials have moved further than what the state is requiring. Bravo for that, however more can and should be done. Pressure should be brought to bear to move the state not just in the direction of more density but toward greater land use as well.

Washington politicians of the past had an obsession with "sprawl" that fueled passage of the Growth Management Act (GMA) of 1990, which in the intervening decades has made Washington's plentiful land into a scarce commodity and priced many residents right out of the real estate market. "[T]he cost and availability of land...today represents approximately 40% of construction costs and home values," the Washington Center for Housing Studies found in a July 2025 report.[64]

The ratio of land to sale prices is so high because of the restraints the GMA puts in place, the report found: "[O]nly 3.74% of Washington's total land area falls within Urban Growth Areas." Outside of those areas, "residential subdivisions, commercial centers and industrial facilities that require urban services are generally prohibited." Through its representatives in Olympia and through its paid lobbying, Spokane ought to push the state to loosen up those restrictions.

Spokane should also avoid a major pitfall that Seattle and many other large cities around the country are falling into. The city government should resist hiking permitting fees to help close a budget gap. That will only slow housing growth and likely cost it more money in the long run.

The Urbanist reported last year on a Seattle permitting fee hike that has now taken effect which "adds an 18% increase on top of a 6.5% adjustment for inflation." This year, homeowners "looking to build a 500-square-foot backyard cottage will pay an additional $543 for permits, and the developer of a 230-unit apartment building will pay an additional $50,000, approximately."[65]

Remember that those numbers do not represent the full freight of permitting fees. Rather, they come in on top of the previous fees. With the 2026 raise factored in, the permitting fees for the Seattle backyard cottage come to about $2,700, for instance. Spokane has more modest fees. Going off of a schedule supplied by the city, permitting for a cottage or granny apartment in Washington's second largest would likely cost just north of $1,000.[66] That's a pretty good selling point in Spokane's favor.

Some of the lessons for Spokane here are obvious for second cities in other states, including their political leadership. For instance, it is ill-advised and often costly to let the state's largest city and its representatives in the state Capitol force you into a big city mold.

Certainly, be open to learning from the successes and failures of other municipalities, but you don't have to be a carbon copy or a suburb. Rather, show some civic pride, figure out what makes your city different and in its own way better than other places that people could choose to live and lean into those strengths.

This is likely to be a far more effective and rewarding approach than trying to keep up with the Seattles.

Here are some other practical ways that might translate into better policy for all second cities:

- Look at other places in your state and nearby states (Spokane is perilously close to Idaho, for instance) where your residents might live instead and find ways to make your city more affordable, or at least more competitive.
- Look at your city's existing housing stock and geography to see what kinds of residential building reforms will fetch the highest returns on effort.
- Approach homelessness in a way that makes sense for your city.
- Take a data-driven, localist approach to crime. Determine where it is occurring. Adjust policing and city laws to reduce violence and property crimes.

Dispatch from a
Small Rust-Belt City:
Hillsdale, Michigan
By Clark S. Judge
WELCOME
TO
e City of
LLSDALE

Dispatch from a Small Rust-Belt City: Hillsdale, Michigan

By Clark S. Judge

The U.S. Census Bureau lists three widely acknowledged classifications for what might be called "demographic clusters": urban, suburban, exurban. Urban and suburban areas are well known, exurban less so. Exurbs exist on the outer edges of metropolitan statistical areas or just outside them.[67]

The Free Cities Center has primarily focused on these three categories of communities and the strengths and weaknesses of their governments, as it looks for market-based solutions and good-government reforms that improve every type of city. As mentioned in the introduction, urban policymakers tend to focus on the biggest cities and metropolitan areas, but smaller cities and towns offer fertile ground for better policies, especially as more Americans flock to some of them.

In recent decades, significant numbers of small towns far removed from Metropolitan Statistical Areas have displayed unexpected potential for vibrancy and growth. This has led some who have worked at strengthening these communities to give them a generic name for their own data gathering and analysis. The name is "agurb."[68]

Hillsdale is one such community. Entirely surrounded by south Michigan farmland, Hillsdale and the adjoining village of Jonesville are rural in mindset as well as geography. That offers both a strength and weakness in dealing with these communities' various challenges.

I learned of this rural attachment at a January 2026 local township[69] meeting. The township's board had called the meeting to hear public comment on the regional power company's plan to install solar panels on extended stretches of local farmland. To power a planned AI data center, the company was offering farmers previously unheard-of amounts of money for the right to cover vast acreage with solar panels.

Hundreds turned out. Passions ran strong. Still, testimony was well-reasoned, well-articulated and respectful of the township supervisors. I felt like I had slipped in on the now famous town meeting that Norman Rockwell portrayed for his 1943 *Saturday Evening Post* cover: "Freedom of Speech" after having lived in a large metro area where such public meetings often turn contentious.

From the simplest to the most polished, one speaker after another spoke of their love of rural life —looking out over the vast fields at sunset, and their closeness to the land growing up. A number had been offered seven-figure payments to give all that up—and turned it down.

The standard of governance in a community as small as the city of Hillsdale (population 8,000 including the students at Hillsdale College) is far more intimate than even moderately sized California municipalities. Yet how this rural "city" has brought itself back from major setbacks and is finding a new direction can offer lessons to much larger cities and towns across the nation.

The Crisis of Hillsdale's Past

Though best known as a college town, in terms of employment, Hillsdale is also a factory town. The college came to Hillsdale in the mid-19th century. The factories—mainly auto industry factories—came as the 20th century began.

First was a home-grown engine producer—Alamo Machine Company, which opened in 1901. In 1931, it merged with another engine maker, creating Hillsdale Machine Shop and Tool Company. For the next 75 years, local autoworkers and their families enjoyed lives of remarkable stability, thanks to Hillsdale Tool and others connected to the auto industry. Many jobs were handed from father to son. The common assumption was that the good days would never end.

Then came 2004. Following unsuccessful union negotiations over restructuring of wages and related issues in the face of rising overseas competition, Hillsdale Tool became the first of four companies to close local operations that year with a couple more leaving in the four years that followed. Together they moved 2,000 jobs in the city's manufacturing sector out of the region.

Some jobs went to China, some to Mexico. A few moved to other states. The lost job count came to roughly one-third of the city's adult population.

The impact was far deeper than many who have written of the Midwest's troubles of the first decade of the 2000s realize. For this article, I interviewed a number of longtime residents active in local affairs, men and women who know the area well. I was often surprised.

For example, I asked a deeply versed community leader about what happened when those "generational jobs" disappeared. We had been discussing the city's alarming, though easily spotted, underclass.

These were men (mainly) lost in drugs and alcohol, not exactly homeless and not exactly employed, sometimes showing up in shelters, but more often camped in the shanty rental housing that characterizes some neighborhoods. His answer: "Children and grandchildren of workers who lost their jobs when the factories left."

Could that be true? I turned to Hillsdale County government's Economic Partnership staff. They gave me these numbers: by 2009 (after the last factory left) unemployment in Hillsdale city hit 17.5%, close to Depression level. The bad days lingered but did not last. By 2024 unemployment was down to a more normal 2.4%.

The exit of factories from 2003 to 2008 was a product of global competition, primarily in the auto industry. But as competition reached beyond the auto industry, moving factories turned out not to be the only way to compete. Another way was redesigning and automating existing plants.

One of Hillsdale's most senior business leaders owns and is CEO of a manufacturing facility, not in the automotive industry. Several decades ago, he grasped where the globalization trends were taking his industry

In response to increasing competition from the Pacific Rim, he started redesigning his company's manufacturing methods. On his own, he developed new manufacturing tools and methods, growing his firm to the third-largest producer in its category in the worldwide industry. His employees are handsomely paid. They have enormous coming-and-going flexibility.

When he started on this path to growth, his company had 500 employees. Today it has 50—with no facilities outside of Hillsdale. Skyrocketing productivity reaches throughout manufacturing in every part of the world. As a result, global employment in manufacturing has declined sharply.

Lesson: Hillsdale cannot live on manufacturing alone. For Hillsdale and agurbs that have gone through a similar ordeal, there is a paradox: the solution to declining employment is more people. An influx of residents brings new ideas, new investments, and new customers and clients.

Opportunity in Hillsdale's Present

For as manufacturing employment declined, service-sector employment grew.[70] Manufacturing involves centralized production and dispersed consumption.

For example, all Ford-150 trucks are assembled in one of two plants: Dearborn, Mich., or Claycomo, Kan.. The number of people who live in Dearborn or Claycomo has no impact on Ford's sales in, for example, Hillsdale.

In contrast, McDonald's hamburgers are "assembled" at each McDonald's restaurant with customers waiting. Restaurants are a service industry. The bigger the local population, the greater the sales and the more people McDonald's can employ, the opposite of manufacturing.

Hillsdale has been part of the national and global shift of employment to services. The city's two largest private employers are in the service sector: the college (700 full-time and part-time staff) and the hospital (520 jobs). One or two major retail outlets came to the area in these years, too.

But by 2025 other changes were gathering like a spring rain on fertile fields. They were changing the town's demographics profoundly and with them the future of Hillsdale and other agurbs with a defining attraction such as Hillsdale has in the college.

"Other Change" No. 1: A New Retiree Generation

Baby Boomers are living longer than did their parents. As a group, they will have more extended, more vigorous, more productive retirements than previous generations. A large proportion want to live near their children and, especially, grandchildren.

At Hillsdale College many faculty and staff have young children and a number of the grandparents of these families have moved nearby, which is exactly what led my wife and me to move after four decades in Washington, D.C.

A college town like Hillsdale is ideal for such couples. The college itself offers a full plate of sporting events, guest lectures, concerts ranging from classical to rock, and theater.

Initially, I thought this demographic shifting was unique to Hillsdale. Then a speaking engagement took me to the University of Virginia in Charlottesville. I told my hostess about what I was seeing in Michigan. She said that she and her husband were seeing the same flocking of retirees to Charlottesville.

Today an outsized portion of college-educated Baby Boomers want to retire, not to specialized retirement communities like Central Florida's The Villages (median age: 74), but to intellectually and culturally stimulating college towns like Hillsdale and Charlottesville, particularly those with athletic teams to cheer on.

The COVID lockdown accelerated this trend. In a May 2024 Census Bureau paper, demographer Luke Rogers explained that with more remote work, "it's likely that some people are more willing to live farther away from their place of employment than they would have in the past."[71]

The affluence and vigor of new retirees migrating to a Hillsdale or a Charlottesville points to a larger and more general change in American life. To the degree that the retirees are not truly retired but sit on boards or continue to work in fields that allow meetings by video conference and briefing papers exchanged by email far from the maddening crowds of major cities is a plus, not a minus.

For two and half centuries, the movement of America was to the West. Pick any number of famous Californians: Ronald Reagan, born in Illinois; Leland Stanford, born in New York; Jack Kerouac, born in Massachusetts. Movement west to east was rare. Now it is common.

And the influx of retirees has a benefit for these college towns in particular, as Hillsdale is demonstrating. "At a time of dwindling U.S. student enrollment, tight school finances and a rapidly aging population, the unusual mashup of schools and senior living is gaining wider appeal," according to *Bloomberg* analyst, Elizabeth Rembert.[72] This trend brings an influx of money and creativity to the city itself.

"Other Change" No. 2: New Technologies

Technology is making small town remoteness even less burdensome to these "retirees" and others working at far-reaching businesses from rural towns and small cities. The equally educated and capable spouses of faculty and senior college employees are harnessing that technology to start businesses and professional practices.

Broadband internet, with its visual and audio capabilities, is ideally suited to moving high-end professional service firms of every variety, to no longer remote communities like Hillsdale. From planning meetings to delivery of product, the difference between maintaining operations in a major city and a town like Hillsdale has largely disappeared. For example, Hillsdale is home to a rapidly growing financial services start-up and a number of creative, innovative, category busting new firms. None would be viable without the internet.

New technology may be on the way to altering physical access to the city. In Hillsdale, the shortness of the local airport's runway (5,000 feet) has been an impediment to establishing commercial air service. But with the recently developed short-takeoff models of regional jets, this barrier may soon vanish. That important as the closest major airline hub, Detroit Metro Airport, is 90 miles away.

Put most simply, demographic and technological trends add up to one conclusion: More than most imagine or understand, Hillsdale and other similarly sized communities are positioned to benefit from the enterprises created by big-city refugees in the decades ahead.

"Other Change" No. 3: Failure of Other Jurisdictions

Migrations of productive, creative people from California to Texas have received plenty of play in the news. Not appreciated is the move elsewhere.

Several decades ago, renowned supply-side economist Arthur Laffer moved his entire consulting practice to Tennessee, which has no state income tax. Ask him and he will list the sins of California government including, but going far beyond, punitive state taxes that drove him and his team away from the West Coast. California is not alone. New York, Massachusetts, Illinois and numerous other states seem bent on outdoing taxing, spending and regulation of the once-Golden State.

The consequence of these intrusions is what it always has been, stultifying energetic creators. For example, in Hillsdale a young entrepreneur from Chicago developed a new and brilliant model for launching a restaurant with minimum capital. He rented an industrial kitchen, adjoining a space that his landlord devotes to a Starbucks-like cafe. Students study in the cafe for hours on end, coffee and pastries next to their laptops.

The young entrepreneur offered a rotating menu of South Asian takeout, fueling the students when they were ready for a full meal. All they needed to do was walk down the hall to his kitchen and select from the day's menu.

Demand was intense. So he had the sales of a restaurateur without paying rent for a restaurant or wages to waiters. The landlord's coffee sales also went up, as students stayed longer, sipping more cups of coffee or tea and munching an additional muffin. Neither the owner of the space nor the young entrepreneur had the capital to open a traditional restaurant. Together they created two thriving businesses.

But why did the young entrepreneur launch in Hillsdale rather than Chicago? The answer can be found any night, any day, by Googling the latest news from Chicago. The online headlines will deliver a list of murders, rapes, robberies and various violent and property crimes. Those go together with taxes and regulations that drive up the cost of doing.

Likewise in California. California is Ground Zero in the nation's affordability crisis on all levels. For example, Sacramento has had a major upscale restaurant boom.[73] Why? Local taxes and regulation on top of squalor and crime have declared war on the creative passions of restauranteurs and chefs. Social dysfunction and outlandish taxes are pricing and regulating many restaurant entrepreneurs out of the San Francisco Bay Area. Many simply moved northeast to the less-troubled state capital.

The consequences not just of high business costs but high living costs have become a key reason for California's exodus cited by public opinion.[74] Ex-Californians nationwide cite their main reason for leaving as home affordability.

Those costs are caused by failed public policy. The Golden State has imposed major impediments to new construction, such as the California Environmental Quality Act (CEQA) and locally approved urban growth boundaries. The result? The median home price statewide is nearly $900,000. The median home price in Hillsdale is $223,000.

Strategy for Hillsdale's Future

In studying his strategic guidance, one of Jack Schultz's principles jumped out at me: "Build [the town's] brand." If the key is to attract people from, say, a 100-mile radius, municipal "branding" will matter.

A great deal has been written, said and done about how towns are or can be branded. At the heart of each story is one "transformative investor" or several.

For a particularly brilliant Midwestern example of the transformative investor, turn the clock back to the 1960s and 1970s and the small town of Columbus, Ind. Columbus was home to an at-the-time modest-sized family business, Cummins Engine, manufacturer of truck motors. Though largely forgotten today, Cummins' principal owner and CEO. J. Irwin Miller, was among the most creative and effective transformative investors in American agurb history.

Miller wanted to attract more capable executives and build a spirit of pride and higher purpose in the town. So, he extended an offer to the town. He and his family's foundation would pay for all architecture and other design-related costs of any new public building, as long as the architect came from a list that he and the foundation assembled.

Columbus now is known as a showcase for the best works of many of the best architects of the period, including Eero Saarinen, I. M. Pei, Robert Venturi, César Pelli and Richard Meier. The buildings alone draw large numbers to Columbus annually. Columbus may be the most imaginatively branded agurb in the nation.

Hillsdale's Transformative Investor No. 1

In the last few years, Hillsdale has found its own versions of J. Irwin Miller, private investors with visions of beautiful and useful spaces that can energize and define a city.

Private investment has been a key to success. Hillsdale has had better financial (and aesthetic) results when private investors have taken the lead. If public money has been used as well, results have been best only after private money has done the initial work and after private investors have reached out and looked very carefully at the strings that go with public money.

An example is Hillsdale's Keefer House Hotel, an historic structure just off Courthouse Square, the town's center. Built in the mid-19th century, the Keefer is an example of what was known as a "railroad hotel." In that era, it provided luxurious relaxation after long train rides. Such gems were features of many small towns along the railroad lines. Today "excursion" trains come to Hillsdale from throughout the Midwest. At least six such railroad companies are active in Michigan, Ohio and Indiana. All are privately backed.

The renovation of the Keefer began with a dentist who, with his wife, moved to Hillsdale from a small town in California. Jeffrey and Marcey Horton had long been dedicated to preserving and reviving classic buildings, but astronomical land prices in and near their California hometown had them looking elsewhere. They were also eager to have their boys in a school dedicated to what is known as "classical learning."

They heard that Hillsdale College had an office for assisting those who wanted to set up classical learning K-12 programs in their hometowns. The college has also established a separate school of education, dedicated to producing classical educators.

The Hortons were captivated by the classic architecture of the Hillsdale's center when they visited the college to discuss bringing classical education to their California town. Soon, Jeff and Marcey had bought a classic home not far from the Courthouse Square, enrolled their sons in the college's K-12 classical academy, and begun considering a renovation-investment strategy. They became the first of Hillsdale's transformative investors at work in the city today.

Their strategy was to make a project of investing their considerable savings in acquiring attractive but badly rundown buildings, investing in basic restoration, then sell them to people or organizations prepared to bring them up to full glory and operate them. After the Keefer, they bought another Courthouse Square gem. In its glory days, the 1919 Dawn Theater was home to vaudeville, silent (and later sound) movies and even opera.

Today the Dawn is again an operating performance and meeting space. In between, the Hortons sold the Keefer to a company that specializes in historic restorations in small Midwestern towns. To help with the second-stage renovation costs, that firm decided to accept an historic restoration grant from the state of Michigan.

Apparently, they did not focus on obligations that came with receiving state support. The grant triggered restrictive rules (for example, only historically authentic bricks could be used in the project). The result was needless delays.

The delays have become a local joke. Word is that the hotel will open soon, but then the current deadline is the fifth so far. Who knows when it will really open its doors?

Advocates (or, by this point, defenders) of the project say that the alternative to state support of renovation was letting an abandoned eyesore sit in the middle of town, scaring away private investors from other projects. The concern about a blighted site deterring further private investment was probably correct at the time the project started. Tradeoffs are part of all complex projects, which even a small, historic and strategically located railroad hotel receiving a measure of public funding will (properly) become. That is not necessarily a criticism of public money and bureaucratic rule of the private investor. It is just a fact of life.

For cities of every size, the issue of government grants and redevelopment activities remains contentious. The Free Cities Center generally looks askance at such subsidies, given the strings attached and its concern of using public dollars for private enterprises.

For example, California eliminated its redevelopment agencies in 2012. Started in the 1940s to combat urban blight, the agencies became a tool for crony capitalism. They diverted public funds from traditional public services and sometimes abused eminent domain.

Hillsdale's Brownfield Redevelopment Authority has avoided many of these pitfalls and focuses, as its name suggests, on upgrading older "brownfield" sites to battle against the abandonment of older buildings.

After the Supreme Court's 2005 *Kelo* decision, which allowed the city of New London, Conn., to use eminent domain to help a pharmaceutical company build a headquarters, Michigan passed a constitutional amendment that largely overturned the decision. As the Michigan Bar Association explained, "Because the Michigan legislature has enacted new, enhanced constitutional and statutory protections against eminent domain abuses, property owners in Michigan enjoy greater rights and protections than those in most other states."[75]

Hillsdale and other small cities will need to wrestle with the subsidy question, but it is clear that their transformation is best driven by private investment and the ideas of locals. The arrival of new residents can help create such projects, as newcomers such as the Hortons often bring a new energy to an older city.

Hillsdale's Transformative Investor No. 2

In the last three years, a second transformative investor has emerged. A graduate of Hillsdale College, Luke Robson is from a family that, like the Hortons, is dedicated to preserving the classic anchors of American culture and faith, emphasizing education and architecture in his work and vision. During his Hillsdale College years, he resolved to rebuild the center of town in a fashion that would preserve of its 19th-century aesthetics.

To succeed, he understood that the part of the city where the 19th- and early 20th-century architecture dominated—the square around the Hillsdale County courthouse—had to become economically self-sustaining. With this in mind, Robson has backed in one space a classic pizza restaurant, in another the town's first truly serious wine store and two other restaurants consistent with the theme.

On the Courthouse Square he has also introduced major office space in buildings renovated consistent with the classic mid-to-late-19th-century aesthetic. None of this work, so far, has been done with public money.

For everything he has achieved already, Robson's transformative investment is just beginning to take form. He has drawn plans for new buildings, all of classical design, that will run along the decayed eastern edge of the Courthouse Square. In those new buildings he plans to establish a totally new trade School of Ecclesiastical Arts.

Robson understands that the great churches and cathedrals of the world will themselves need restoration in the coming century—and that the last generation of stone masons, crafters of stained glass, and others in trades that made and maintained these cathedrals, churches and schools glorious have not been replaced as they have retired in recent decades.

These artists are dying out—and their skills with them. Robson will soon break ground on his new trade school. Talk is in the air of attracting schools for other trades—from culinary to digital—to take space on the Hillsdale Courthouse Square. As the great urban theorist Jane Jacobs wrote, "new ideas need old buildings."

Hillsdale's Future: Encouraging Competing Models for a New Age

The core question: How can cities such as Hillsdale promote the kind of private-sector growth that is the key to their revival? Here there is a need for a deep dive into Hillsdale's reputation as a difficult place to start businesses.

Local officials and business owners have told me that it is particularly hard to build a new company in Hillsdale. Why, I asked? Do we need faster approval of permits? Are there too many permits? Are there unseen barriers in law, city government culture or other areas?

Numerous think tanks and academics have made comparative studies ranking states for their regulatory and tax environment toward new and small businesses. I picked three of these studies: the Mercatus Center (2024), the Pacific Research Institute (2015) and the Cato Institute (2022). All are libertarian or conservative think tanks. The findings: Michigan ranked 38th of the 50 states in the Mercatus report, 28th in PRI's and 12th in the CATO study.[76]

In other words, in these academic studies Michigan consistently fell in the middle of the pack. That did not match the strident indictment of local scuttlebutt. Why? I looked at the methodologies of the three probes. All focused on the details of the regulations themselves. I asked, did anyone focus on the norms of enforcement?

An online search turned up a San Francisco tech-based home and office services company called Thumbtack. In 2021, Thumbtack in partnership with the Kauffman Foundation (which focuses on understanding the challenges to small businesses) polled 3,600 small business owners in all 50 states.[77] They asked for an A-F grading of the state's regulatory burden. Michigan received an F.

To its credit, since 2021 Michigan has attempted to do something about this. In 2021 Gov. Gretchen Whitmer issued an executive order that "require[s] state government to reimburse applicants for missed deadlines, where possible. It will lower costs and ensure permits for more projects of all kinds—housing, community revitalization, manufacturing, clean energy, and water protection—get done on time while protecting our air, land and water."[78]

One state official I interviewed has since told me that Michigan's enforcement remains spread across many offices in Lansing (the state's capital) and elsewhere. In contrast, he said, Ohio has a single drop box address for all regulatory submissions.

In Hillsdale and throughout Michigan, speed, simplicity and responsiveness in administration seem to be missing ingredients in the state's relationship with the small-and medium-sized firms on which smaller towns—agurbs—will depend more heavily than major metropolitan areas for their futures.

Housekeeping in a House Divided

When I started this project, a veteran of agurb renewals told me that the one thing all successes had in common—the factions of a town put away their differences and worked together. "We have never done that," this leader said.

When I started attending City Council meetings, a recurring complaint was the $100,000 the airport lost annually. One faction in town saw the airport as a playground for wealthy parents of students at the college. But then the airport manager retired.

Replacing her was an entrepreneur who had started and built the region's most prominent flight school. Like his predecessor, he knew aviation. Unlike her, he knew the numbers that guided the aviation industry—costs, alternatives to do the same job cheaper and better, potential new sources of revenue. Within four months, the airport was at breakeven.

My sense is that if that kind of managerial audit were to be applied to every aspect of city government the divisions in the city would diminish. For example, the city maintains a ride-up-on-call service. According to city records, it loses something like $72,000 per year. Resentment to it runs soft, if at all. But the success of the airport audit suggests that an audit of that service might enable closing that gap, too.

The tensions in the city fall into familiar categories: town v. gown; those who struggle v. those who don't, or at least don't as much. I won't go into all of the fault lines.

My view is that tightening management of city services, and using savings to salve areas of irritation—for example road maintenance—would reduce tensions, as would a season of small business rebirth.

The city is years behind in keeping up its roads, for which it charges a large fee when the repair work passes by a home. Every organization needs a shaking out now and then. A real house cleaning could give the city resources for repair, not just of roads, but in many areas.

So would opening a series of first-class trade schools in and around the county Courthouse Square. Recruit, for example, the Culinary Institute of America[79] to open a branch in Hillsdale. Would Cirque du Soleil set up training center? Or the automotive oriented Lincoln Technical Institute?

Through the college, Hillsdale is already branded as a center of education. How about extending the brand by making it a center for the new wave of education—and opening to the non-college-bound young people of Hillsdale a road to hope? It's time for such thought experiments in Hillsdale and elsewhere.

Endnotes

1   Census Bureau, "Metropolitan and Micropolitan Statistical Areas Population Totals: 2020-2024," March 2025, https://www.census.gov/data/tables/time-series/demo/popest/2020s-total-metro-and-micro-statistical-areas.html.

2   Andrew Van Dam, "Wait, is America a nation of small towns?" *The Washington Post*, June 13, 2025, https://www.washingtonpost.com/business/2025/06/13/wait-is-america-nation-small-towns/.

3   Addison Del Mastro, "'Urbanism' Isn't Synonymous With 'Big City,'" *Strong Towns*, May 11, 2021, https://archive.strongtowns.org/journal/2021/5/13/urbanism-isnt-synonymous-with-big-city.

4   "Population of the largest metropolitan areas in the United States," Statista, accessed Feb. 15, 2026, https://www.statista.com/statistics/183600/population-of-metropolitan-areas-in-the-us/?srsltid=AfmBOorLGJpk0jtT21B6XMNLMkudcPUD7RVHtybrLGoh4ULtVxSQWcdq.

5   Dan Walters, "San Joaquin Valley: California's poor stepchild?" *CalMatters*, Feb. 24, 2019, https://calmatters.org/commentary/2019/02/san-joaquin-valley-californias-poor-stepchild/.

6   Mark Bittman, "Everyone Eats There," *The New York Times Magazine,* Oct. 10, 2012, https://www.nytimes.com/2012/10/14/magazine/californias-central-valley-land-of-a-billion-vegetables.html?src=me&ref=general.

7   Staff, "California's San Joaquin Valley: A Region in Transition," Congressional Research Service, Dec. 12, 2005, www.everycrsreport.com/reports/RL33184.html.

8   Staff, "Armor-Clad Mayor Asks City: 'Who's Willing To Fight For Stockton?'" CBS News, May 16, 2013, www.cbsnews.com/sacramento/news/armor-clad-mayor-asks-city-whos-willing-to-fight-for-stockton/.

9   Staff, "Stockton Mayor Anthony Silva's series of scandals," ABC10, Oct. 4, 2018, www.abc10.com/article/news/local/stockton-mayor-anthony-silvas-series-of-scandals-update/103-601003124.

10   Gillian Edevane, "Stockton Mayor Considers Adopting Program That Pays Criminals Not To Shoot People," NBC Bay Area, July 6, 2017, https://www.nbcbayarea.com/news/local/stockton-mayor-considers-adopting-program-that-pays-criminals-not-to-shoot-people/25329/.

11   Andrea Riquier, "Can Stockton's groundbreaking guaranteed income experiment help solve the affordability crisis?" *Stockton Record*, Nov. 20, 2025, https://www.recordnet.com/story/news/politics/government/2025/11/20/universal-basic-income-is-having-a-moment-stockton-helped-lead-the-way/87344787007/.

12   Tim Anaya, "Is Stockton's Basic Income Scheme Actually Working?," *Right by the Bay*, March 10, 2021, https://www.pacificresearch.org/is-stocktons-basic-income-scheme-actually-working/.

13   Damon Dunn, *Punting Poverty: Breaking the Chains of Welfare* (San Francisco: Pacific Research Institute, 2020), 31.

14   "Stockton on My Mind," HBO, https://www.hbomax.com/movies/stockton-on-my-mind/bad9ba2b-3b78-49ab-9c25-1ec26796884d.

15   David Siders, "The Fall of Michael Tubbs," *Politico*, Dec. 23, 2020, https://www.politico.com/news/magazine/2020/12/23/the-fall-of-michael-tubbs-449619.

16   Ibid.

17   San Joaquin County Registrar of Voters registration statistics, accessed Feb. 15, 2026, https://www.sjgov.org/department/rov/office/registration-statistics.

18   City of Stockton, Mayor Christina Fugazi bio, accessed Feb. 15, 2026, https://www.stocktonca.gov/government/city_council/mayor.php.

19   Kelly Curran, "Housing Prices Fall 13.8% in 2008," *Housing Wire*, Feb. 10, 2009, https://www.housingwire.com/articles/home-prices-fall-138-percent-2008-report/.

20   Harris Kenny, "What Happened in Stockton?" Reason Public Policy Foundation, June 27, 2012, https://reason.org/commentary/what-happened-in-stockton/.

21   Staff, "How Stockton went broke: A 15-year spending binge," *Reuters*, July 4, 2012, https://www.reuters.com/article/stockton-bankruptcy-cause/rpt-how-stockton-went-broke-a-15-year-spending-binge-idUSL2E8I406L20120704/.

22   Ibid.

23   Harris Kenny, "What Happened in Stockton?" Reason Public Policy Foundation, June 27, 2012, https://reason.org/commentary/what-happened-in-stockton/.

24   Editorial, "Stockton ruling affirms a skewed perspective," *The Orange County Register*, April 3, 2013, https://www.ocregister.com/2013/04/03/editorial-stockton-ruling-affirms-a-skewed-perspective/.

25   Wes Bowers, "Stockton ranked one of most fiscally solvent cities in US," *Stockton Record*, May 22, 2018, https://www.recordnet.com/story/news/politics/county/2018/05/22/stockton-ranked-one-most-fiscally/12158038007/.

26   Staff, "City Reports 2026," Truth in Accounting, accessed Feb. 15, 2026, https://www.truthinaccounting.org/resources/page/city-reports.

27   Steven Greenhut, "Formerly bankrupt Stockton is fiscally healthy again, but offers warning to others," California Policy Center, June 12, 2018, https://californiapolicycenter.org/formerly-bankrupt-stockton-is-fiscally-healthy-again-but-offers-warning-to-others/.

28   Steven Greenhut, "Testimony in opposition to legislation to revive crony capitalist redevelopment agencies," California Assembly Committee on Housing and Community Development, April 24, 2024, https://www.rstreet.org/outreach/testimony-in-opposition-to-legislation-to-revive-crony-capitalist-redevelopment-agencies/.

29   Rev. Jim Conn, "Stockton Bankruptcy: Fat City's Missed Opportunities," *Capital & Main*, July 3, 2012, https://capitalandmain.com/stockton-bankruptcy-fat-citys-missed-opportunities.

30   Ariella Cohen, "On the Waterfront, A Bankrupt City," *Next City*, June 27, 2012, nextcity.org/urbanist-news/on-the-waterfront-a-bankrupt-city.

31   Alison Vekshin, "The Building Boom That's Sinking Stockton," *Bloomberg*, April 12, 2012, www.bloomberg.com/news/articles/2012-04-12/the-building-boom-thats-sinking-stockton.

32   Michael Fitzgerald, "Cost overruns for New City hall show a need for change," *Stocktonia*, Sept. 9, 2025https://stocktonia.org/news/opinion/2025/09/09/mike-fitzgerald-the-buildings-that-ate-stocktons-money/.

33   Daniel Thigpen, "Waterfront hotel renamed," *Stockton Record*, May 4, 2011, https://www.recordnet.com/story/business/2011/05/04/waterfront-hotel-renamed/50063755007/.

34   Diana Marcum, "Stockton cops fighting city hall," *Los Angeles Times*, Dec. 29, 2011, https://www.latimes.com/archives/la-xpm-2011-dec-29-la-me-stockton-20111229-story.html.

35   Tim Arango, "A California City Grieves Over a Shooting at a Toddler's Birthday Party," *The New York Times,* Jan. 4, 2026, https://www.nytimes.com/2026/01/04/us/stockton-california-shooting-birthday-party.html.

36   Office of Gov. Gavin Newsom, statement on Stockton shooting, Dec. 23, 2025, www.gov.ca.gov/2025/12/23/governor-newsom-deploys-dedicated-teams-to-fight-crime-in-stockton-building-on-existing-successful-partnerships/.

37   California Association of Realtors, "Data and Statistics," accessed Feb. 15, 2026, https://www.car.org/marketdata/data.

38   Steven Greenhut, "Anaheim's freedom experiment still offers lessons for cities," Free Cities Center, Sept. 17, 2022, https://www.pacificresearch.org/anaheims-freedom-experiment-still-offers-lessons-to-cities-2/.

39   World Population Review, "Tacoma, Washington Population 2025," accessed Jan. 6, 2026, https://worldpopulationreview.com/us-cities/washington/tacoma.

40   World Population Review, "Spokane, Washington Population 2025," accessed Jan. 6, 2026, https://worldpopulationreview.com/us-cities/washington/spokane.

41   "About," NIKE 3ON3, accessed Jan. 6, 2026, https://www.nike3on3.com/about.html.

42   Corbin Vanderby, "Hoopfest Nets over 800 Injuries, down from Previous Years," *The Spokesman-Review,* June 29, 2025, https://www.spokesman.com/stories/2025/jun/29/hoopfest-nets-over-800-injuries-down-from-previous/.

43   "Riverfront Park Spokane - Explore Nature in an Urban Setting," VisitSpokane.com, accessed Jan. 6, 2026, https://www.visitspokane.com/things-to-do/recreation/parks/riverfront-park/.

44   Jessica Fisher, "Spokane Is the Birthplace of Father's Day," City
      of Spokane, June 18, 2020, https://my.spokanecity.org/news/sto-
      ries/2020/06/18/spokane-is-the-birthplace-of-fathers-day/.

45   Nate Sanford, "Where Does the Camp Hope Money Go?," *The
      Inlander*, Jan. 11, 2023, https://www.inlander.com/news/where-
      does-the-camp-hope-money-go/article_c96bdaf2-55c7-5681-8ce0-
      86344192d2d5.html.

46   Daniel Walters, "Camp Hope Officials Say They Repeatedly Asked
      Police for Help Removing Dangerous Residents—That Help Rarely
      Came," *The Inlander*, March 29, 2023, https://www.inlander.com/
      news/camp-hope-officials-say-they-repeatedly-asked-police-for-
      help-removing-dangerous-residents-that-help/article_2911684a-
      c086-5da7-aff4-c3382da48042.html.

47   *Jewels Helping Hands v. Hansen*, No. 102814-8 (Wash. Apr.
      17, 2025), https://law.justia.com/cases/washington/su-
      preme-court/2025/102-814-8.html.

48   Celina Van Hyning, "City of Spokane Asks Judge to Declare I-90
      Homeless Camp a Chronic Nuisance, Authorize Warrant of Abate-
      ment," KREM2, https://www.krem.com/article/news/local/home-
      less/camp-hope-chronic-nuisance-complaint-spokane-wsdot/293-
      39365133-291a-44e7-9528-c7fe8e2836d1.

49   RaeLynn Ricarte, "Spokane Police Chief Joins Movement to Empty
      Homeless Camp," *The Center Square*, Oct. 10, 2022, https://www.
      thecentersquare.com/washington/article_35fef9f6-48d5-11ed-b476-
      c33a922aabde.html.

50   Garrett Cabeza, "Two People Burned in Camp Hope Propane
      Explosion," *The Spokesman-Review*, March 17, 2023, https://www.
      spokesman.com/stories/2023/mar/17/two-people-burned-in-camp-
      hope-propane-explosion/.

51 Brian Coddington, "Judge Declares Camp A Nuisance Property," City of Spokane, March 24, 2023, https://my.spokanecity.org/news/releases/2023/03/24/judge-declares-camp-a-nuisance-property/.

52 Marbut, Robert G., Jr., *Survey and Data Analysis of the Street-Level Homelessness Community within Spokane*, Spokane Business Association, June 2025, https://spokanebusinessassociation.com/wp-content/uploads/2025/10/Marbut-Spokane-Final-Report.pdf.

53 Matthew B. Anderson et al., *2025 Point-in-Time Count Homelessness in Spokane: The Broader Context* (City of Spokane Department of Community, Human, and Health Services, 2025), https://static.spokanecity.org/documents/chhs/hmis/reports/2025-point-in-time-count-report-the-broader-context.pdf.

54 RaeLynn Ricarte, "Spokane Councilor: Forcing Cops, Not Firefighters to Buy Electric Cars Is 'Double-Standard,'" *The Center Square*, March 29, 2022, https://www.thecentersquare.com/washington/article_9afacf1a-afab-11ec-bc7f-036190e995a5.html.

55 RaeLynn Ricarte, "Spokane Council Censures Bingle, Asks Mayor to Ban Him from City Hall," *The Center Square*, Feb. 1, 2022, https://www.thecentersquare.com/washington/article_399e4bf2-83aa-11ec-b796-e7cbc7d8ea61.html.

56 Erin Sellers, "Spokane City Council Keeps Staff and the Public Alike in the Dark at Budget Meetings," *RANGE Media*, Nov. 20, 2025, https://rangemedia.co/city-budget-meetings-inaccessible/.

57 Jewels Helping Hands v. Hansen, No. 102814-8, slip op. (Wash. Apr. 17, 2025), https://www.courts.wa.gov/opinions/pdf/1028148.pdf.

58 Redfin, "Washington Housing Market: House Prices & Trends," Redfin.com, updated Nov. 2025, accessed Jan. 6, 2026, https://www.redfin.com/state/Washington/housing-market.

59   Redfin, "Spokane Housing Market: House Prices & Trends," Redfin.
      com, updated November 2025, accessed Jan. 6, 2026, https://www.
      redfin.com/city/17154/WA/Spokane/housing-market.

60   "Building Opportunity," City of Spokane, accessed Jan. 6, 2026,
      https://my.spokanecity.org/projects/shaping-spokane-housing/build-
      ing-opportunity-for-housing/.

61   Anthony Gill, "Spokane Leads the Way with Parking Reform,"
      The Urbanist (blog), July 14, 2023, https://www.theurbanist.
      org/2023/07/14/parking-reform-in-spokane/.

62   Lisa Gardner, "Spokane City Council Passes Historic Camping and
      Obstruction Ordinance," City of Spokane, Oct. 28, 2025, https://
      my.spokanecity.org/news/releases/2025/10/28/spokane-city-coun-
      cil-passes-historic-camping-and-obstruction-ordinance/.

63   Tim Clouser, "Spokane Delays $1M Grant over Condition Re-
      quiring Compliance with Trump Agenda," *The Center Square*, Jan.
      13, 2026, https://www.thecentersquare.com/washington/arti-
      cle_2ef057c2-e364-48a8-93fc-30ca39c648e0.html.

64   Riley Helean, "How Land Limits Contribute to Washington's Hous-
      ing Crisis," More Homes, Higher Prices (Washington Center for
      Housing Studies, Building Industry Association of Washington, July
      17, 2025), https://housingstudies.biaw.com/reports/how-land-lim-
      its-contribute-to-washingtons-housing-crisis.

65   Ryan Packer, "The 'Structural Change' About to Make Homebuild-
      ing More Expensive in Seattle," *The Urbanist*, Nov. 18, 2025, https://
      www.theurbanist.org/2025/11/18/structural-change-about-to-make-
      new-housing-more-expensive-in-seattle/.

66   City of Spokane, Building Permit Fee Schedule (Spokane, WA:
      Department of Building Services, City of Spokane, n.d.), https://
      static.spokanecity.org/documents/business/commercial/permit-fees/
      building-permit-fee-schedule.pdf.

67   From Wikipedia: "The word *exurb* (a portmanteau of *ex-tra [outside]* and *urban*) was coined by Auguste Comte Spectorsky, in his 1955 book *The Exurbanites*, to describe the ring of prosperous communities beyond the suburbs, that are commuter towns for an urban area. In other uses, the term has expanded to include popular extraurban districts which nonetheless may have poor transportation and underdeveloped economies due to their distance from the urban center." Exurbs can be defined in terms of population density across the extended urban area.

68   Jack Schultz, *Boomtown: 7 ½ Keys to Big Success in Small Towns,* see page xiii for explanation of the term "agurb", which the author coined.

69   Michigan townships are a unit of government created by the Northwest Ordinance of 1787. Township governance coexists with city, and county governments. Each township has defined taxing and regulating authority and responsibilities for schooling and elements of public safety and welfare.

70   Staff, Federal Reserve Bank of St. Louis, "All Employees, Goods Producing," accessed Feb. 15, 2026, https://fred.stlouisfed.org/series/USGOOD.

71   Lindsay Spell and Marc Perry, "More Exurban Communities Now Among Nation's Fastest Growing Places," U.S. Census Bureau, May 16, 2024, https://www.census.gov/library/stories/2024/05/exurbs-city-population.html.

72   *Bloomberg* video, Colleges Tap Boomers' Wealth by Building Senior Living on Campus July 19, 2025, https://www.bloomberg.com/news/videos/2025-07-19/colleges-tap-boomers-wealth-by-building-senior-living-on-campus.

73   Ella Quittner, "How Sacramento Turned Into a Great Restaurant City," *The New York Times*, Dec. 5, 2023, https://www.nytimes.com/2023/12/05/dining/sacramento-restaurants.html.

74 Mary K. Jacob, "Golden State's housing crisis laid bare as skyrocketing prices force Californians to flee in record numbers." *New York Post,* https://nypost.com/2026/01/26/real-estate/sky-rocketing-housing-prices-force-californians-to-flee-in-droves/.

75 Jerome Pesick and Ronald E. Reynolds, "Recent Changes in Eminent Domain Law," *Real Property Law*, the Michigan Bar Association, November 2007, https://www.michbar.org/file/barjournal/article/documents/pdf4article1242.pdf.

76 Paul McLaughlin and Dustin Chambers, "Snaphot of State Regulations, 2024," the Mercatus Center, Aug. 6, 2024, https://www.mercatus.org/regsnapshots24; Wayne Winegarden, "The 50-State Small Business Regulation Index," the Pacific Research Institute, July 2015, https://www.pacificresearch.org/wp-content/uploads/2017/04/SmBusinessIndex_UpdatedVersion2_web.pdf; "Freedom in the 50 States," the Cato Institute, 2022, https://www.freedominthe50states.org/regulatory.

77 Andrew Heritage, "2021 Small Business Friendliness Survey," Thumbtack, https://blog.thumbtack.com/our-10th-annual-small-business-friendliness-survey-29efaa6f5b#.

78 Office of Gov. Gretchen Whitmer, "Gov. Whitmer Signs Executive Directive to Speed Up State Permitting, Making Michigan More Competitive," Aug. 3, 2023, https://www.michigan.gov/whitmer/news/press-releases/2023/08/03/whitmer-signs-executive-directive-to-speed-up-state-permitting.

79 CIA Campuses, Culinary Institute of America, accessed Feb. 15, 2025, https://www.ciachef.edu/cia-campuses/.

About the Authors

Steven Greenhut

Steven Greenhut is a longtime journalist who has covered California politics since 1998. He wrote this book for the San Francisco-based Pacific Research Institute, where he founded that think tank's Sacramento-based journalism center in 2009 and is director of its Free Cities Center. He currently is western region director for the R Street Institute, a Washington, D.C.-based free-market think tank, and is on the editorial board of the Southern California News Group. Greenhut has worked full-time as a columnist for *The Orange County Register* and *The San Diego Union-Tribune*. He writes weekly for *American Spectator* and *Reason* magazines. He is the editor of the PRI book *Saving California*, and the author of *Winning the Water Wars, Abuse of Power* and *Plunder*. He is also the author of the Free Cities Center booklets *Back from Dystopia: A New Vision for Western Cities; Putting Customers First: Re-Envisioning our Approach to Transportation Planning; Giving Housing Supply a Boost: How to Improve Afford ability and Reduce Homelessness* (with Dr. Wayne Winegarden); *Building Cities from Scratch: America's Long History of Urban Experimentation;* and *Is There a War on Suburbia? Calling a Truce in the Battle Over Land Use.*

Clark S. Judge

As Managing Director of the White House Writers Group, Clark Judge provides strategic communications counsel to clients in industries ranging from financial services to transportation to high technology.

Judge has assisted some of the nation's most prominent businesses in developing public positions and communications strategies for responding to regulatory challenges, promoting legislation, marketing high-end professional services, and pursuing mergers and acquisitions. For political clients he has written numerous nationally televised speeches, primarily during presidential campaigns.

In the White House, Clark Judge served as Speechwriter and Special Assistant to both President Ronald Reagan and Vice President George Bush.

After two-and-a-half years serving the Vice President, he joined President Reagan's speechwriting staff in 1986 and remained with Mr. Reagan through the end of his term. A member of the Moscow Summit speechwriting team, he was also the lead writer for the Toronto Economic Summit in 1988 and helped shape the White House approach to the 1988 presidential campaign.

A Harvard M.B.A., Judge was a business consultant and writer in New York prior to his first government assignments, which concerned urban policy and international economic policy.

He has written on national and international issues for *The Wall Street Journal* and other publications. He is chairman of the board of the Pacific Research Institute.

Jeremy Lott

Jeremy Lott is a longtime resident of the Evergreen State. After a childhood set in Tacoma, he now lives in Lynden, near the Canadian border, with his wife and two children. Lott is a former small business owner and former Washington editor for a newswire. As bureau chief, he oversaw extensive coverage of Olympia, Seattle and Spokane and hosted the podcast, "Washington in Focus."

Lott's writing has been published and republished widely, in more than 1,000 outlets. He is the author of and collaborator on several books for adults and children. These include *The Warm Bucket Brigade*, a history of the American vice presidency; *I'll Never Forget It*, memoirs of the late Maryland Gov. Marvin Mandel; *Your World-Class Assistant,* a leadership book from Michael Hyatt; the *Movie Men* comic book, with artist Doug Curtis; and, most recently, *The Three Feral Pigs and the Vegan Wolf,* with artist Paula Richey.

About Pacific Research Institute

The Pacific Research Institute (PRI) champions freedom, opportunity, and personal responsibility by advancing free-market policy solutions. It provides practical solutions for the policy issues that impact the daily lives of all Americans, and demonstrates why the free market is more effective than the government at providing the important results we all seek: good schools, quality health care, a clean environment, and a robust economy.

Founded in 1979 and based in San Francisco, PRI is a non-profit, non-partisan organization supported by private contributions. Its activities include publications, public events, media commentary, community leadership, legislative testimony, and academic outreach.

Center for Business and Economics

PRI shows how the entrepreneurial spirit—the engine of economic growth and opportunity—is stifled by onerous taxes, regulations, and lawsuits. It advances policy reforms that promote a robust economy, consumer choice, and innovation.

Center for Education

PRI works to restore to all parents the basic right to choose the best educational opportunities for their children. Through research and grassroots outreach, PRI promotes parental choice in education, high academic standards, teacher quality, charter schools, and school-finance reform.

Center for the Environment

PRI reveals the dramatic and long-term trend toward a cleaner, healthier environment. It also examines and promotes the essential ingredients for abundant resources and environmental quality: property rights, markets, local action, and private initiative.

Center for Health Care

PRI demonstrates why a single-payer Canadian model would be detrimental to the health care of all Americans. It proposes market-based reforms that would improve affordability, access, quality, and consumer choice.

Center for California Reform

The Center for California Reform seeks to reinvigorate California's entrepreneurial self-reliant traditions. It champions solutions in education, business, and the environment that work to advance prosperity and opportunity for all the state's residents.

Center for Medical Economics and Innovation

The Center for Medical Economics and Innovation aims to educate policymakers, regulators, health care professionals, the media, and the public on the critical role that new technologies play in improving health and accelerating economic growth.

Free Cities Center

The Free Cities Center cultivates innovative ideas to improve our cities and urban life based around freedom and property rights – not government.